Ravenscourt
B·O·O·K·S

The Father of Television

By

Jane Davin

Mc Graw Hill **SRA**

Columbus, OH

Photos: 21, Hulton Archive/Getty Images, Inc.;
39, © Bettmann/Corbis; **60,** © Bettmann/Corbis.

Illustrations: Denny Bond

SRAonline.com

 SRA

Send all inquiries to this address:
SRA/McGraw-Hill
4400 Easton Commons
Columbus, OH 43219

Printed in the United States of America.

ISBN: 978-0-07-611303-3
MHID: 0-07-611303-5

   3 4 5 6 7 8 9 MAL 13 12 11 10 09 08

The McGraw-Hill Companies

Contents

Introduction

The story you are about to read is true. Parts of it may seem like a drama made for television. Some parts are heartwarming. Other parts may seem like a comedy. At times, it may even seem like part game show.

Like the 1960s game show *To Tell the Truth,* the history of television could show three contestants standing on a stage. The lights come up on the first man. He says, "I am the father of television." The lights go up on the second man. He also says, "I am the father of television." The lights go up on the third man, who also claims, "I am the father of television."

The panel, led by game show host Bill Cullen, would try to figure out which man is telling the truth. Then the host would say, "Will the real father of television please stand up?"

You will learn about Philo "Phil" Farnsworth and his amazing Image Dissector. You will meet David Sarnoff, a man of false faces and dreams.

You will also meet a Russian named Vladimir Zworykin. He invented two important parts to the television system: the Kinescope and the Iconoscope.

What are these things? Who are these men? What are their stories? What do they have to do with television and its beginnings? Tune in and find out.

—Chapter 1—

Watching Is Learning

"We can't run this ranch without a generator," Uncle Albert said. "I just got it back from the shop a few weeks ago, and it's broken again!"

In 1918, Farnsworth and his family shared a 240-acre farm with his uncle, Albert. Farnsworth was 12 years old at the time. One generator provided all the electricity for two houses. It also powered all the farm buildings on the sprawling ranch near Rigby, Idaho.

A local repairman, William Tall, often went to the ranch to do odd jobs. He also worked on electrical machines. Farnsworth would quietly watch as Tall worked. Farnsworth was interested in how electricity worked.

He learned a great deal watching Tall fix things. Tall wasn't interested in electricity outside of fixing the machines. But Farnsworth was amazed by the power of electricity. What electricity could do and how it worked were unlike anything he had imagined. He wanted to learn all he could about this amazing thing called electricity.

Uncle Albert kept complaining about the generator. So Farnsworth got up his courage and said, "I think I can fix it, Uncle Albert. May I try?"

There were a few laughs and jokes from Farnsworth's cousins. But Farnsworth's father, Lewis, said, "Al, why don't we let Phil try? It won't hurt anything. Our only other choice is to go buy another generator. We can't afford that."

"Okay, see what you can do with this old thing," Uncle Albert said. Then he stood back. He gave his sons, Farnsworth's cousins, his familiar frown. This told them to behave themselves.

Farnsworth ran to the tool shed to get kerosene and rags. He had often seen Tall use kerosene to clean parts. When Farnsworth returned, he opened the dented, rusty can of kerosene. He dabbed some of it onto a clean rag. He wiped off all the grime that had built up on the important wires and metal parts in the generator. He also cleaned many of the smaller parts. Then Farnsworth took apart the generator. He tuned parts as he had seen Tall do many times. Then he put all the parts back together. Farnsworth stood straight up and admired his finishing touches to the generator.

He turned around and was surprised to see a larger group watching him. Agnes and Laura, his sisters, had come from the house. Laura's eyes were glued to Farnsworth's project as she wiped an apple with her apron. Its red skin soon gleamed. Farnsworth's younger brothers, Carl and Lincoln, had come from the barn. The two brothers watched as if Farnsworth were a genius. Farnsworth's cousins stood by, watching closely. They were more than a little interested in all this.

Farnsworth wiped his hands on the dirty rag. Then he said, "I think we can press the button and see if it works."

Uncle Albert gave him a nod and a wave with his work-worn fingers. Farnsworth pushed the button. The generator started up right away, whirring like a brand-new machine. Beaming, Farnsworth looked at his father. Lewis quickly hugged his son. Everyone cheered.

Uncle Albert patted Farnsworth on the back, laughing with joy. Farnsworth's sisters both giggled. They playfully snapped the suspenders on Farnsworth's back.

Then Laura stepped back and shouted, "Phil, catch!" She tossed him her shiny apple. Farnsworth caught it and looked down at the polished red skin. Without another thought, he sank his teeth into the sweet apple.

*Everyone turned to go back to the jobs of the day. But the sound of the well-running generator remained in the air. The whirring generator was music to the whole family.

"I could've done that," one of Farnsworth's cousins said. The other two cousins laughed loudly. Then they teased him all the way back to the barn.

That was a special day for Farnsworth. From then on he was the official fix-it guy on the farm. He was young for such a title. But he seemed to have a gift for knowing what to do with electrical things.

His gift, however, was a matter of interest and reading. In his attic bedroom, Farnsworth had found a treasure of dusty old science and engineering magazines. What luck! He read dozens of these magazines.

He learned all he could about magnets and electricity. He wondered what could be invented with electricity.

In* 1921 Farnsworth's family moved to a 140-acre ranch just down the road from Uncle Albert's. Even though he was still very young, Farnsworth set up his family's farm with electricity. He also picked up scrap wires, boxes, and magnets to make a lab for himself. That way he could work on more electrical projects.

He improved life for his sister Agnes too. She worked hard every day. She had to turn the handle on the washing machine by hand. So Farnsworth found a way to put a motor on the handle so it turned by itself. This made Agnes even happier than the day Farnsworth fixed the generator.

Farnsworth also made his mother's sewing machine run on electricity. She could sew faster and easier. But his mother was not pleased. She was used to hard work. The foot pedals on her sewing machine were an important part of what she had always known. So she asked him to undo the electrical parts from her sewing machine. Farnsworth did as he was told.

Be the First One on Your Block!

In one of the science magazines, Farnsworth saw an ad for building "your own crystal radio." He ordered the parts for the radio. The kit included wood wound with copper. There was also a box of crystals for picking up radio waves, which were then turned into electricity. Knobs, antennas, and a headset completed the kit.

During the 1920s, nothing was more exciting to a kid than building a radio. Picking up radio signals from one's own yard was the best! For Farnsworth, this was exciting. But it sparked this young inventor's imagination for something better. What if a *picture* could be sent from one place to another? In the most unlikely of places, Farnsworth was about to figure out how to do it. Farnsworth saw into the future while plowing his potato field.

—Chapter 2—

The Dream of Television

*By the time Farnsworth was 14, working with wires and magnets was second nature to him. While plowing, he had time to think about what he wanted to invent. This is where he did a lot of dreaming. Farming was not his job of choice, but he worked hard because it helped his father and mother.

One day Farnsworth was thinking about an inventor he had read about. The inventor, Paul Nipkow, had invented a machine that could transmit a live scene. It used a spinning black disk with pin holes poked in it. Light passed from the scene through these holes. The light was then turned into electricity that was passed along a wire. The electricity would cause light to shine through pin holes in another rotating disk at the other end of the wire. This would reproduce the scene scanned by the original disk.

Farnsworth knew this disk* would never work well. It could never spin fast enough for details from the scene to show clearly. He also knew that electrical and magnetic activity moved faster than anything anyone had thought of so far. So how could he make a television that would work well?

First Farnsworth needed to scan the image. *Scanning* means reading—like the way you are reading this page. But electric scanning is millions of times faster than eye scanning.

Farnsworth thought electron beams might be the answer. He knew electron beams could be caught and sent. He had read about Karl Braun, who had sent electron beams through an airless glass tube in 1897. Farnsworth wanted to find a way for electricity, magnets, and light to work together. Maybe with a tube he could make a picture "travel."

Farnsworth steered the horses in straight lines in the potato field. Suddenly he stopped and turned around. He looked at all the straight rows he had plowed. They had been plowed one at a time, row by row. Farnsworth wondered what would happen if light from an image was caught and passed through a tube. Maybe electron beams could be sent through a tube in a single line. In a magnetic field, these beams could be lined up in an orderly way. Magnets could very quickly pull the electrons from side to side, thousands of times a second. Together the tiny lines would make an image. The picture would look like his rows of potatoes. But the rows would be much smaller, of course. There would be hundreds of them in every inch.

This idea excited Farnsworth. He couldn't wait to tell his father what he had been thinking. Lewis knew that his son was very bright. He agreed this was a great idea. So he talked to his son about protecting that idea.

Patents Are for Protecting

"When you come up with an idea," Lewis told Farnsworth, "it is very important that you protect it. You need to get a patent on it. A *patent* is a legal note. It states that an idea is yours alone. A patent is, in a way, your own property. For example, no one can just come to our farm and dig up our potatoes. They are potatoes that we worked hard to plant. In the same way, no one else can take your great ideas when you have a patent. Do you see why this is important?"

Farnsworth thought for a moment. Then he said, "If I invented something that people could use, and even needed, and were willing to buy . . . well, yes! I can really see now why having a patent is important."

"That's right, Phil," his father said. "An invention is like brain property. Some people are interested in making a lot of money. Some are not honest. They might steal what you have. They could say it was their idea. Without a patent, how would you prove that you thought of it first?"

"I see, Father. This idea I have for images traveling from one place to another, line by line, could be a big discovery. Maybe one day we will have more than just radio signals traveling through the air. Maybe images will travel too. Think of it, Father!"

"That would be amazing. I am so proud of you, son," Lewis said. "Let's make sure to keep this idea top secret. It needs to be signed on paper as yours and yours alone."

"Okay, Father. I won't tell anyone. Hey, how do the potato rows look?"

"Straight as light from a glass tube!" Lewis said, smiling. He and Farnsworth laughed as they headed back to the house for supper.

Go to the Head of the Class, Phil!

Farnsworth was too young to take the science classes he wanted. He was just a ninth grader. Only 12th graders could take those classes. Mr. Tolman, the science teacher, agreed to meet with him after school. When they met, Farnsworth asked Mr. Tolman many good and important questions. The teacher saw that Farnsworth was not just any bright student.

Soon Farnsworth was allowed in class. He even spoke in front of the class. He explained ideas young Albert Einstein had about light speed and time. This was a very bold thing for a ninth grader to be talking about. But inventing television would take a person with a great mind. It would take someone who was willing to "think outside of the box." Einstein had one of those minds. So did Thomas Edison. And so did Farnsworth.

In time, Farnsworth shared some of his lines-of-light ideas with Mr. Tolman. The teacher was impressed with this amazing student. He knew that big things lay ahead for Farnsworth.

—Chapter 3—

RCA

In the 1920s, Farnsworth continued to work on his invention. Another man was also working on dreams of his own. That man was Sarnoff. He grew up poor in Russia. Sarnoff hoped to live in the United States. But he wanted more than just a good life. He wanted to be rich and famous.

His family did move to the United States, where Sarnoff delivered newspapers. He was also a messenger. Soon he met G. Marconi, the inventor of the wireless telegraph and the radio. Marconi's wireless telegraph sent messages in dots and dashes through the air. Sarnoff became Marconi's helper. He was determined to be a great man like Marconi.

David Sarnoff in 1933

It's funny how greatness rests on people. For some, it fits like a well-made suit. It makes sense. For Marconi, his wireless telegraph invention proved his greatness. For Farnsworth, brains and hard work showed greatness to come. For Sarnoff, however, fame would be hard-won. In time, there would be many questions surrounding his greatness.

In 1926 Sarnoff got a better job. He became a wireless telegraph operator at Marconi's company. He made $7.50 a week. He was 20 years old.

It is widely known that Sarnoff often told tall tales about his deeds. He was known to take credit for things in which he played only a small part.

The *Titanic* sank on April 14, 1912. Sarnoff was on duty that night. *He told many people that he was the only message link between the *Titanic* and the rest of the world. That was a pretty big claim. Actually, he was just one of many wireless operators on duty that night.

A few years later, RCA—the Radio Corporation of America—was formed. Ed Nally was president of RCA. Sarnoff became Nally's first assistant. Up to this time, radios were only used by the government. They sent or tracked war messages. There were no radios for listening to music.

But soon, RCA owned over 2,000 patents. This company wanted to be on the cutting edge of all wireless radio. It bought patents for any invention that had to do with radios. This made RCA very powerful. No other company could match or do business equal to RCA. Sarnoff was now one of RCA's leading men. He would quickly become even more powerful.*

The Beauty of Being First

Do you know what it feels like to be first in a race? If you don't play sports, maybe you know what it's like to figure out how a story or a puzzle ends before anyone else. Or maybe, like Farnsworth, you know what it's like to do something special.

Imagine you are living in the 1920s. There are no televisions. The only radios are used to help pass on urgent messages for the U.S. government. There is electricity, but it is a rare treat to anyone living outside of a large city. Just think of all the inventions yet to come. One day there will be radios that broadcast music and sports. There will be televisions, stereos, tapes, CDs, DVDs, computers, and cell phones. You might want to invent something that runs on electricity. It would be nice to be the first. What would you invent?

In the 1920s, ideas proven to work meant money in a person's pocket. One person might invent a new kind of antenna. Another might invent a radio box that was easier to use. Yet another person might invent something to make radio signals stronger. The signals could then reach faraway places. Each invention was made by someone willing to sell his or her patent rights to RCA. Selling patents for money was not strange in the 1920s. RCA collected the patents and became the leader in all parts of electronic systems.

Until then, radio was not used for pleasure. It was first used during World War I. At that time government messages could be sent by radio over long distances. But RCA's goal was to make radio entertaining. And they had an even bigger goal. They wanted to claim the invention of television.

Sarnoff liked taking credit for things. He worked very hard to make RCA come in first. Then, as one of its main spokesmen, he would also be first. This was a way he could meet his own goal in life—to be a great man!

Sarnoff was part of the first public radio broadcast. It was not just signals for government purposes. This broadcast was entertainment! But this meant radio signals had to be able to reach many nearby towns at the same time. The signals had to travel up to 500 miles. Newspapers were more than ready to cover the event. Nothing like it had ever been done before.

RCA made radio history on July 2, 1921. A boxing match between G. Carpentier and heavyweight champion Jack Dempsey was aired. In Jersey City, New Jersey, 90,000 people bought tickets to see the amazing match. Boxing fans got their money's worth. The big news, though, was that over 300,000 more fans could also listen to it on the radio.

Much was done to make this first radio broadcast of a sporting event a success. Tickets were sold. Radios were sold. Word got out about the event. When the big night arrived, it was a huge success. Sarnoff, of course, said he had managed the whole event. But that wasn't true. This was just like the *Titanic* story. Sarnoff had bent the spotlight toward himself. He had taken credit that wasn't his. He was really just one of many radio operators that helped make the event possible.

After this first program, RCA and Sarnoff became more powerful. RCA owned all the patents for the equipment needed to run a radio station. They even owned patents for building radios! RCA had a tight grip on radios and radio parts. Smaller radio companies couldn't succeed. If they got parts, tools, and airtime illegally, RCA took them to court.

One good thing Sarnoff did was sell patent rights and tools to smaller radio companies. In exchange, RCA got part of their profits. In this way, RCA could make even more money.

—Chapter 4—

Farnsworth's Company

In 1926, Farnsworth turned his tiny lab into a company of his own. He now worked in San Francisco, California, at 202 Green Street. He continued to be the main inventor. But he had other smart people working in the lab and on the business end. Farnsworth's company was small. He could not afford all the experiments needed to complete his television system.

RCA, on the other hand, had lots of money to hire the best engineers and inventors. The race was for a big prize: inventing television. Sarnoff did not think Farnsworth was a threat. Was he?

On January 7, 1927, Farnsworth filed papers to get a patent on his "television system." He was finally ready to try out his new camera tube. He called it his *Image Dissector.* By September 27 of the same year, Farnsworth was 21 years old. He had married his high school sweetheart, Elma "Pem" Gardner. Gardner was very important to Farnsworth's dream of inventing television. Gardner worked with Farnsworth and his two business partners, George Everson and Leslie Gorrell.

Could Farnsworth turn a dream into a real invention? Creating a clear image from a camera tube would be a huge news item! The press would jump to cover this story. Television invented by a man who didn't even work for RCA!

*Just a few years earlier, Zworykin, a Russian engineer, had arrived on the scene. In 1923 he had tried to get a patent on a television system of his own. Zworykin worked at a company named Westinghouse. He said he was able to send and produce on a screen an image of a cross. But he had no written proof. Also, the men he had shown his system to at Westinghouse did not think it worked. Zworykin himself said that sending an image caused some problems. By 1934 the patent office agreed that his machine didn't work.

But Zworykin invented one thing that did work. It was a way of storing a picture while it was being scanned. Zworykin had invented a piece of the television puzzle in 1929 called the *Kinescope*. But the invention of television was still years off. Someone needed to find a way to make it* work.

In 1929 Farnsworth's company was struggling because of the stock market crash. That was the year that most of the United States' money markets failed. Rich people lost a lot of money. Middle-income people became poor. Poor people became even poorer. Zworykin had visited Sarnoff at RCA. He told Sarnoff how close he was to inventing television. Sarnoff was interested, and he and Zworykin began a business relationship. Together, they hoped to win the race for inventing television.

Sarnoff quietly hired Zworykin from Westinghouse. They planned a visit to Farnsworth's lab. They thought Farnsworth might be willing to give Westinghouse permission to use some of his patents.

Foxes in the Hen House

What really took place was spying. Zworykin and Sarnoff wanted to see how Farnsworth's television system was made. How might Zworykin take Farnsworth's ideas and add them to his own? If he could do that, RCA might win the television race.

Like letting a fox into a hen house, Farnsworth opened his lab to Zworykin in April 1930. Farnsworth thought Zworykin had come as Westinghouse's best man. Farnsworth and his wife even invited Zworykin to their home for dinner. Farnsworth planned to let Westinghouse use his patents. He wasn't ready to sell his company to them, though. Even so, he was excited to speak with a fellow inventor whom he respected. He showed Zworykin many parts of the lab. He showed him how his latest inventions worked. Zworykin took notes on everything Farnsworth was willing to show him.

Farnsworth had no reason to think Zworykin was spying. He didn't know Zworykin was trying to win the television race. And he had no idea that Zworykin had any tie to Sarnoff. The television race was about to get ugly.

After the three-day visit, Farnsworth's lawyers discovered that Zworykin's visit wasn't business as usual. Right away, Farnsworth's company took RCA to court. They said RCA had broken a law of trust.

Sarnoff wasn't worried. He continued to get the best inventors to work for RCA. He pushed harder to have someone invent a clear televised image. RCA was now losing money due to the stock market crash. Still, Sarnoff wanted more than anything to win the television race. He would not be beaten by some nobody from San Francisco!

Then, in August 1930, the patent that Farnsworth worked to get in 1927 was finally accepted. Farnsworth's television scanning system, patent #1,773,980, and his television receiving system, patent #1,773,981, were issued. His work had been tested and was proven to work! It didn't matter whether Zworykin had stolen Farnsworth's ideas or not. Farnsworth's patent was official. He was the official inventor of television! Right? But wait. This story is not finished yet.

Zworykin, with Sarnoff's help, soon brought his own lawsuit forward. Zworykin claimed he had invented a camera called the *Iconoscope* that made a clear picture. The Iconoscope worked, Zworykin said, because of the system he had invented back in 1923. So the original television idea should be stated as being from 1923, the year of his failed patent.

Add to this the trouble Farnsworth had because his company was small. He had far less money than RCA. They could hire the best inventors and own the most products. Farnsworth couldn't. He knew he could never win as a producer of television. So he set his sights on one thing. He wanted credit as the inventor of television. But Zworykin and Sarnoff would not give in without a fight.

Prove It!

The court held that if someone said they invented something, they had to prove that it worked. A television system had to scan, or gather, a picture. This system had to send the picture somewhere. Then the picture must show up somewhere else on a screen.

Zworykin could not get around the fact that his first try had failed. In 1923 he could not prove that his invention worked. In 1927 Farnsworth proved that his did. The strength of Farnsworth's case lay with the truth. His television idea had been proven. His patent was issued in 1930. The famous court case #64,027, *Phil Farnsworth v. Vladimir Zworykin,* was closed in 1934. At age 29, Farnsworth was declared by law the inventor of television. His battle was won. Or was it?

Television would be the tool Sarnoff would use to blur the edges of truth once again. But this time, Sarnoff would take his bows on a much larger stage. He would put himself in front of a lot more people.

Television sets would soon be in the homes of trusting Americans. Farnsworth might have won his battle. But Sarnoff would soon get his face on the television screen. He was out to win a war.

It was clear who had invented television. Now a new set of problems arose. Farnsworth knew his company was not large enough to take television to its next level. Television was almost ready to become a useful tool in homes across America. RCA wanted to make televisions for the public. But it needed Farnsworth's license permission. And Farnsworth needed RCA's supplies.

Sarnoff did not like that they needed Farnsworth's license. RCA, and Sarnoff, had never before had to ask someone's permission for anything. But if RCA wanted to make televisions, there was no other way. Being named among the "Outstanding Young Men of 1939" by a well-known writer, Farnsworth would not be ignored.

Philo T. Farnsworth with his television transmitter

The 1939 World's Fair

In 1939 the theme of the World's Fair in New York was "Building the World of Tomorrow." Sarnoff went public at the fair. He put RCA, and himself, forward as the power behind television. He ignored Farnsworth's patent rights. He made speeches and showed the latest televisions. People could even go in front of a television camera and get an "I was televised" card at the fair. Sarnoff put his own face on the television screen at the World's Fair. Nowhere was Farnsworth's name spoken. Sarnoff gave the false idea that he was the brain behind this amazing machine. Using Farnsworth's own invention, he put Farnsworth into the shadows. Would people ever find out the truth about the invention of television?

After Sarnoff's World's Fair performance, Farnsworth's company took RCA back to court. They were breaking laws again! But RCA was ready to get televisions into stores. They did not want any more bad news going around about them. Plus, they didn't want court problems stopping them. So they agreed to pay Farnsworth one million dollars. They also offered Farnsworth money for every television sold. In exchange, they asked permission to use Farnsworth's license. It was the first time RCA ever paid another company for the right to use its property.

This was a great success for Farnsworth. But as time went on, he became sad. He knew that television would be used to bend the truth as well as to tell the truth. Truth or lies would depend on the face on the screen.

World War II Halts Television

The attack on Pearl Harbor in 1941 shook the United States. Japan's raid on U.S. ships pulled the United States into World War II. Making television sets for home use came to a screeching halt. The war was now more important than any box for entertainment.

Farnsworth would not see any money from RCA until after the war. At that time, patents only lasted 17 years. This meant trouble for Farnsworth. Just two years after the war, in 1947, his patent for television ended. That meant that anyone, including RCA, could use his ideas without his permission. It looked as though television, and any money from RCA, would be out of Farnsworth's hands forever.

—Chapter 5—

Baby Steps

By 1946 World War II had ended. Most of the first television sets were made by RCA. They cost 385 dollars each. By 1948 television shows were reaching a million homes. Television was taking its first baby steps. The first kids' program was a puppet show on WBKB-TV in Chicago called *Kukla, Fran, and Ollie*. Fran, a real woman, would speak with her puppet friends, Kukla and Ollie. Kukla was a clown. Ollie was a one-toothed dragon. Many say these puppets looked much like *Sesame Street* characters.

News reporters were few. They included Mike Wallace, Hugh Downs, and the most famous of early television reporters, Edward R. Murrow. A live show starring Ed Sullivan began on CBS. On NBC, Milton Berle did a show called *Texaco Star Theater*.

Showdown

In the late 1950s and the 1960s, television westerns included *Wyatt Earp, Bonanza,* and *Gunsmoke*. If Farnsworth and Sarnoff had been cowboys, they could have dueled at high noon about television. Their battles of pride were the stuff westerns are made of.

Sarnoff produced a strange program that aired on January 7, 1949. NBC aired *Television's 25th Anniversary Special*. People scratched their heads.

Televisions had only been out for three years. But Sarnoff wanted to honor Zworykin's patent—the one he tried for in 1923, the one he didn't get. Sarnoff told the story of television from his own point of view. He called Zworykin the "inventor of television." No words about Farnsworth were spoken.

About a year later Sarnoff called many radio and television makers, pushing to have himself given the title "Father of Television." RCA agreed. No one questioned it.

The only time Farnsworth was seen on television was on a 1950s game show called *I've Got a Secret*. He was the secret guest. He said his name was "Dr. X." The panel thought he might be a medical doctor. He was good-humored. But no one really knew who he was. By the end of the show people did know. But his face and his place in the public mind remained in the shadows of Sarnoff and Zworykin.

Jack LaLanne

In the late 1950s and early 1960s, television programming grew. An exercise show was hosted by a fit, pep-talking man named Jack LaLanne.

Dressed in a blue jumpsuit, LaLanne guided his television audience through sit-ups, simple stretches, and tips on staying fit.

How Do We Look, America?

Television became a mirror held up to the face of America in the 1950s and early 1960s. Programs showed the dreams and views of Caucasian people in the United States. Programs did not show the dreams and views of people of other races.

This was the time after World War II, when men had come home from the war. They went back to work in factories or offices.

*Women were no longer needed for wartime factory work. Time seemed to turn back to the late 1800s. Women were suddenly the "weaker gender" once again.

Television shows were created around this idea. June Cleaver in *Leave It to Beaver* and Harriet Nelson of *Ozzie and Harriet* were just a few of the perfect, pie-baking moms of 1950s television. In only a few shows did a woman get to be wacky or interesting, like Samantha in *Bewitched*.

Men were the heads of their homes once again—at least on television. Ward Cleaver almost always had the daily bit of wisdom to give his sons, Wally and Theodore. Men went off to work, provided for their families, and got to do a lot more stuff than women. They were detectives, like Mike Connors in *Mannix*. They were scuba-diving crime solvers, like Lloyd Bridges in *Sea Hunt*. Jack Webb from *Dragnet* was* another detective who had a no-frills way of dealing with women witnesses.

"You Rang?"

As 1960s television grew, ideas for programs became more creative and bold. *The Addams Family* was a funny show about a loving but creepy family. The Addams family handled everyday situations like most families, but they were cheerfully gruesome about it. They were fond of all things creepy. They lived in a squeaking house. When a bell rope was pulled, Lurch, the butler, would ask in a low and scary voice, "You rang?"

President Kennedy

Three important events from the 1960s were covered on television. They serve as landmarks in the lives of U.S. citizens. On November 22, 1963, President John F. Kennedy was shot and killed, shocking the United States and the world. Film played on television gave people a powerful picture of this sad event.

A few days later, President Kennedy's funeral was shown on television.

The Beatles

In 1964 an English rock group, The Beatles, became an overnight sensation. Soon after, they were on *The Ed Sullivan Show*. This event was probably the biggest night ever for *The Ed Sullivan Show*. Young people in the studio audience could hardly stay in their seats because the excitement was so high. *The Ed Sullivan Show* was a favorite Sunday evening program of millions of Americans.

One Small Step, One Giant Leap

An event that Farnsworth thought was the best of television was the moon landing in July 1969. He was proud to have invented the tool that allowed people to view Neil Armstrong's foot planted in the dusty surface of the moon.

Armstrong's words, "One small step for a man, one giant leap for mankind," were heard all over the world.

As the 1960s came to a close, a new era in television was about to begin. Television soon created programs that made people laugh, cry, and think harder about important issues. It became a teaching tool too. The nightly news showed the joys and dramas of history as it unfolded. Television ads became a huge business. Companies worked hard to get their products on television. Television was shaping what people thought and what they bought.

Television was no longer in the hands of one, two, or even several people. Thousands of hands in front of and behind the cameras shaped the path of television.

—Chapter 6—

Television's Growth

All in the Family

Television shows became bolder about issues in everyday life. The United States' struggle with race problems was addressed in the television comedy *All In the Family*. Archie Bunker, a brash-talking, narrow-minded Caucasian man, sat in his easy chair, solving the problems of the world. He squirmed and tried to be polite when his new African American neighbors came over to shake hands and say hello. This show held a mirror up to the United States in the 1970s. It caused people to think and talk with one another about race issues, families, and our changing world.

Sesame Street

Sesame Street has long been a powerful teaching tool for kids of all ages. Its high-quality script makes use of Jim Henson's famous puppets. On *Sesame Street,* real people like Bob, Maria, Gordon, and others visit with these fuzzy friends. They talk, share, and solve problems together.

The Oprah Winfrey Show

Daytime television talk shows and their hosts invited guests and the studio audience in to chat. At the end of the 20th century, television was used for helping people as well as for entertaining them. *The Oprah Winfrey Show* has covered important issues such as parenting, education, and money. It has become the most popular daytime talk show in history.

Kent State

In the 1970s, television became a sharper voice of agreement and disagreement with modern life. While the Vietnam War was still raging, nightly footage of the fighting was on the three major television networks. In the United States, one strong image was seen on the news. This was when U.S. soldiers came to Kent State University in Ohio to control riots. Four unarmed students were killed. Two of them were protesting the war. Seeing it on television wasn't like reading about it in a newspaper. Television had caught the sad images of students lying wounded or dead on the university grounds.

Space Shuttle Disaster

Many times television has been the bearer of bad news. In 1985 the space shuttle *Challenger* exploded in the air shortly after liftoff. This was shown on live television, and people in the United States mourned. This was the first space trip to include a person who was not an astronaut. Christa McAuliffe, a teacher, was one of the crew. She and all others on board died in the accident.

Sports

Sports programs have changed in the last 40 years. Television now covers national sports events, the Olympics, and local sports. The three major networks broadcast all over the nation. But they also "feed" stories to local stations. Every major city has its own tie to ABC, NBC, or CBS.

9/11

On September 11, 2001, live morning news shows began another normal day. Then, all things that were normal stopped. People in the United States watched on live television as terrorists destroyed the World Trade Center in New York City. The Pentagon in Washington, D.C., was also attacked. The terrorists used airplanes as weapons. Thousands of innocent people died that day. In a matter of 15 minutes, America's feeling of safety changed for good. Before and since 9/11, television has been a tool to inform, warn, and guide people.

Reality Television

In the early 1990s, America saw the beginning of what is known as "reality television." One show might involve scary or disgusting events. Another might call for cooking better than anyone else in the kitchen. On *Survivor*, strangers are put together in "deserted island" situations. They must "rough it," using tree branches and leaves to make their homes. They are given few supplies and must share with one another.

Cable

*Cable television has grown into a huge broadcast business in the last 15 years. Now, with cable bringing programs into homes, ABC, NBC, and CBS have to share the television audience. Cable channels offer everything, including sports, music, health, nature, and history.

More people having computers in their homes has changed television too. The current image clarity is called high-definition television. And, for many, the television itself will soon be a thing of the past. Perhaps one day people will be able to buy a product that is one complete system for televisions, computers, digital audio systems, and cell phones.

Farnsworth would be proud and probably amazed to see how his original ideas have improved over the last 35 years. Being the true inventor that he was, Farnsworth would most likely want to be involved in the latest inventions of the 21st century. He died in March 1971, however, so* he didn't get to see these modern improvements.

Sometimes It Takes a Group of Kids

Not long ago, students at a grade school in Utah were studying Farnsworth's life. Because he was born in Utah, they were very interested in his life and work. Then they read the whole story about him. They knew that his name had been lost in the history of television.

So this bright group of youngsters wrote to the U.S. government. They found out that in the U.S. Capitol building, two statues could be displayed for each of the 50 states. There was only one statue from Utah. It was a statue of Brigham Young, the man who founded Utah. The students got busy. They worked hard to get the word out. Soon these students were able to get the U.S. government to allow the second statue from Utah.

In 1990 a gathering was held at the U.S. Capitol in Farnsworth's honor. They honored his contributions and invention of television. Pem, Farnsworth's widow, and her three sons, Philo, Kent, and Russell, attended this event.

A second bronze statue now stands in the halls of the U.S. Capitol. The statue is of Farnsworth looking down at a television tube in his hands, his beautiful Image Dissector. Under the statue are the words "Father of Television."

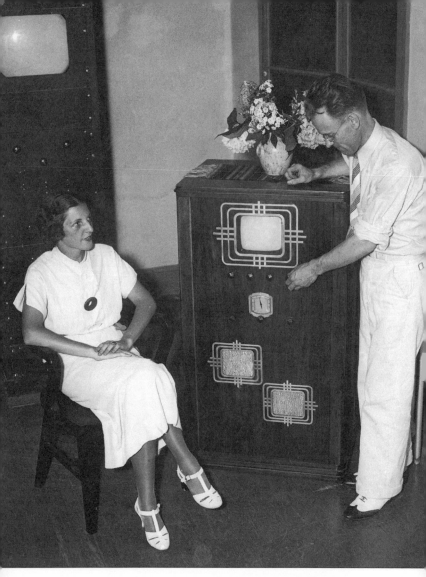

Farnsworth tunes his combination
radio and television set